GREAT BUILDINGS

THE
PARTHENON

Peter Chrisp

RSVP
RAINTREE
STECK-VAUGHN
PUBLISHERS
The Steck-Vaughn Company

Austin, Texas

GREAT BUILDINGS

THE COLOSSEUM

THE EMPIRE STATE BUILDING

THE GREAT PYRAMID

THE HOUSES OF PARLIAMENT

THE PARTHENON

THE TAJ MAHAL

Published by Raintree Steck-Vaughn Publishers, an imprint of Steck-Vaughn Company

Library of Congress Cataloging-in-Publication Data
Chrisp, Peter.
The parthenon / Peter Chrisp.
    p.   cm.—(Great buildings)
    Includes bibliographical references and index.
    Summary: Discusses the history, construction and many uses of the Parthenon in Greece.
    ISBN 0-8172-4917-6
    1. Greece, Ancient—Juvenile literature.
    [1. Greece, Ancient. 2. Architecture.]
    I. Title. II. Series.

Printed in Italy. Bound in the United States.
1 2 3 4 5 6 7 8 9 0 01 00 99 98 97

Illustrations: Mike White and Clive Spong
Map: Peter Bull

CONTENTS

▲ Animal sacrifice was important to the ancient Greeks. They believed the smoke from the roasting meat carried their offerings up to the gods. This carving from the Parthenon shows sacrificial animals on their way to the altar on Athene's birthday.

ATHENA'S BIRTHDAY PARTY

It was the birthday of the goddess Athena, protector of the city of Athens. Thousands of Athenians made their way in a procession to the Acropolis, or "high city." This rocky hill was a holy place where the most important temples stood. Towering over the Acropolis itself was a marble temple to Athena called the Parthenon.

In the center of the procession was a cart, shaped like a boat with a tall mast, from which a bright yellow piece of cloth hung like a sail. The cloth was a new robe, woven for the ancient wooden statue of Athena that was housed on the Acropolis. It was her birthday present.

The Athenians climbed the hill, leading a hundred oxen and sheep, which were also gifts for Athena. They were led to the altar, a high platform near the Parthenon. One by one, the animals' throats were cut. Some of the meat was burned at the altar; the rest was roasted over open fires for the people. This was a treat, for they rarely ate meat. As they sat enjoying their picnic, they looked up at their beautiful temple, the Parthenon, its milky-white marble shining in the sun.

CHAPTER ONE

ATHENS AND ANCIENT GREECE

▼ As part of their system of democracy, the Athenians held open-air meetings on a hill called the Pnyx, west of the Acropolis. Here all the citizens could speak in debates and decide laws by voting.

The ancient Greeks never belonged to a single nation. For more than 650 years, from about 1000 B.C., every Greek lived in a polis, one of the hundreds of city-states on the Greek mainland or on the islands and coasts of the Mediterranean Sea. The Greeks said that their city-states were scattered about the Mediterranean like frogs sitting around a pond. The tiniest was the island of Delos, with just 2 sq. mi. (5 km²) of land. Athens ruled over the land of Attica, which at 1,000 sq. mi. (2,600 km²), was one of the biggest.

◀ Each city state had its protector among the gods. This relief was carved on the occasion of an Athenian decree honoring the city state of Samos. It shows Hera, protector of Samos, on the left, with the goddess Athena of Athens.

Each city-state had its own government and laws. Athens invented a system called democracy, meaning "people power." Every citizen of Athens had a say in how the city-state was governed. Citizens also served as judges, lawyers, and juries in trials. In wartime, they became soldiers.

Only men born of Athenian parents were citizens. Women were not citizens, and neither were men who had come to Athens from other Greek cities. There were also thousands of slaves—men and women who had no rights at all. They had been captured in wars, bought from foreign slave traders, or brought up in Athens as the children of slave parents. Of the 300,000 people who lived in Attica, only one in six was an Athenian citizen.

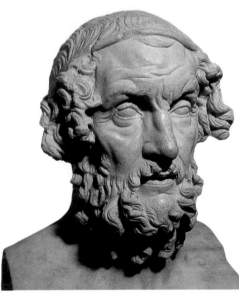

Greece is a land of long, dry summers and mild winters. The fine weather allowed Greek men to spend much of their time outside, with their fellow men. The heart of Athens was the agora, or marketplace, where the men met each day to argue about politics and law cases or just to chat.

Greek men were very competitive. Rival city-states were always quarreling and going to war with one another. Within each city, the men all tried to outdo one another. Athenian playwrights and poets competed for prizes.

▲ A Roman bust of the Greek poet Homer, who is thought to have written two famous long poems, *The Iliad* and *The Odyssey*, more than 2,500 years ago. These poems were recited from memory in competitions at religious festivals. Homer was so important to the ancient Greeks that he was known simply as "the Poet."

▶ This carving shows a woman preparing grain for making bread in ancient Greece, in the fifth century B.C.

Artists and architects tried to make more beautiful works than their rivals. Every speaker in the public meetings wanted to make the best speech. Everything was seen as a competition.

While Greek men spent most of their days outside, women mostly stayed indoors. They spun wool and wove it into clothes. They looked after children and gave orders to the household slaves. Their one public role was to serve goddesses, like Athena, as priestesses.

Games and sports

This detail from a jar, called an amphora, shows a chariot race. Sports were very important to the ancient Greeks. The festivals in honor of the gods usually included contests, such as running and chariot racing. The Greeks loved watching these races and believed that their gods enjoyed them too. The most famous games of all were held at Olympia in honor of Zeus, ruler of all gods. These multisport games are still held today—the Olympic Games have become a worldwide event, held every four years.

"Women are better than men. They care for the home and look after goods brought over the sea. Without a wife, no home is clean and prosperous. As to religion, we women play the most important role.... Women conduct rites for the goddesses which would be unholy for men to perform."

A female character from a play by Athenian playwright Euripides

▼ This detail from a cup illustrates the Greek myth of Athena's birth. Hephaestus, god of fire and metalworkers, has just split open the head of Zeus, seen here holding his thunderbolts. According to legend, Athena sprang from Zeus' head, fully grown and armed with a shield.

The Athenians worshiped many different gods whose temples could be found all over Attica. The temple of Poseidon, god of the sea, for example, stood at Cape Sounion, overlooking the waves. The goddess of wheat, Demeter, was worshiped at Eleusis, 10 mi. (16 km) west of Athens.

To the Athenians, the most important of all the gods was Athena, goddess of wisdom, war, and crafts. She was believed to have shown the Athenians how to grow their most important crop, the olive tree. She invented the potter's wheel and taught women how to weave. She gave her name to the city, which belonged to her.

There was an old story about how the land had come to belong to Athena. People said that there had once been a contest between Athena and Poseidon. The two gods met on the Acropolis, where each claimed the right to rule Attica. The local people had to choose between the two gods. Poseidon struck the Acropolis rock a great blow with his trident. Immediately, seawater began to flow from the hole. This meant that Poseidon was offering the city power over the sea. Then Athena lightly touched the rock with her pole and the first olive tree sprouted. This was her gift to the city, and it won the contest.

The Athenians knew exactly where the two gods had stood when they met on the Acropolis. There was still a mark in the rock left by Poseidon's trident. Athena's sacred olive tree still grew there.

▼ Athena is seen as the goddess of war in this bronze statue. In her warrior form, she was known as Athena Promachus, "she who fights in the front ranks."

Greek mythology

The ancient Greeks believed their many gods were part of a large family. The gods of Greek mythology had many human characteristics, but they were immortal and immensely powerful. Zeus was the most powerful god, as he ruled the sky and earth. His brothers also had their own kingdoms: Poseidon ruled the sea and Hades the underworld, or kingdom of the dead. All the gods had areas, such as music, fire, and hunting, which they represented or taught to humans. The Greeks had many myths about the antics of their gods, who fought and competed among themselves as well as looking after humans.

▼ A Greek soldier, called a hoplite (or foot soldier), is shown in this picture from a vase, painted around 480 B.C. Scenes of war, like many other aspects of life in ancient Greece, were used to decorate jars and dishes of all kinds.

CHAPTER TWO

THE GREEKS AND THE PERSIANS

Between 558 and 500 B.C., the Persians—the people of the country that is now Iran—conquered the biggest empire the world had known. It stretched from Egypt to the borders of India and had taken over the eastern Greek cities. More than 40 million people lived under Persian rule.

Unlike Athenian citizens, who governed themselves, everybody in the Persian Empire had to obey the will of the king. The Athenians thought that this was as bad as being a slave. So when the eastern Greeks rose up against the Persians, in 499 B.C., the Athenians sent a fleet of warships to help them. Despite this help, the Greek uprising was crushed.

The Persian king Darius now wanted to punish Athens. In 490 B.C., he sent an invasion force of 600 ships to the plain of Marathon, northeast of Athens. The Athenian army rushed to Marathon where, greatly outnumbered, they decided

> "The Athenians were triumphant, chasing the enemy, and cutting them down until they reached the sea, and men were calling for fire and taking hold of the ships."
>
> Herodotus the historian, describing the battle at Marathon.

to attack. Gripping their shields, they charged down the hillside toward the Persians. It was an amazing victory for the Athenians: Some 6,400 Persians were killed, but the Athenians lost only 192 men.

The Athenians were certain that their success was due to the help of their goddess, Athena. To celebrate and to thank her, they decided to build a big new temple on the Acropolis. It was called the temple of Athena Parthenos ("the virgin"), or the Parthenon.

▲ The court of Darius the Great is shown on this relief. Standing behind the throne is Xerxes, the son of Darius who succeeded him as king.

◄ Greek warriors battle with Persians on this monument from Asia Minor. The Greeks called all foreigners "barbarians," people whose speech sounded meaningless, like the sounds "bar-bar-bar." The Persians were considered the worst barbarians of all.

The defeat at Marathon was a terrible disaster for
the Persians. When the news reached their empire,
there were more uprisings against Persian rule.
These kept the Persians busy for almost ten years.
However, in 480 B.C., the Persians invaded Greece
again, this time to conquer the whole country.
Their new king, Xerxes, son of Darius, led an
army that was so big that it seemed unbeatable.

As the Persians marched toward Athens, the
Athenians, with no chance against the huge army,
abandoned their city. They crossed in ships to the
neighboring island of Salamis, taking with them
their most prized possession, the wooden statue
of Athena. Finding Athens deserted, the Persians
set fire to it. They destroyed the temples on the
Acropolis, including the half-built Parthenon.
From Salamis, the Athenians could have seen
their city go up in flames.

Xerxes now sent his huge fleet against the
Athenians at Salamis. The Greek ships were
outnumbered, but they were faster and had bronze
battering rams. The Greek ships darted between

◀ A warship shown in a mosaic from ancient Greece. At the prow is the battering ram with which enemy ships were attacked.

the slow Persian ships, snapping their oars and ramming them. Xerxes watched in horror as his fleet was destroyed.

The Athenians returned to their city and began to rebuild their homes. But they did not repair the temples—the ruins were left as a reminder of the terrible behavior of the Persians. There was one piece of good news: Athena's sacred olive tree had not been killed by the fire. From its blackened branches, it put out new green leaves, a sign that the goddess was still watching over Athens.

▼ This lion devouring a calf is thought to be a carving from the pediment of the original Parthenon, which was ruined by the Persians when they invaded the deserted city of Athens.

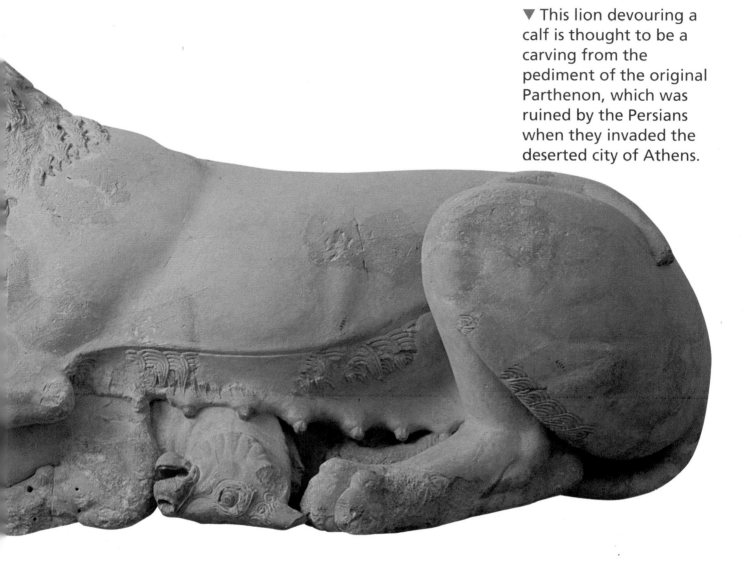

After Salamis, it was the turn of the Greeks to go on the offensive. In 478 B.C., they held a great meeting on the tiny island of Delos. It was attended by Greeks from hundreds of city-states, mostly from the eastern islands. They agreed to join together in a league to attack Persia.

Each member of the League of Delos promised to give something to build up a great war fleet. The Athenians had already shown their skill at winning sea battles, and they had the biggest fleet. Many city-states found it simpler to give money rather than to build their own ships. As a result, Athens supplied the ships, the soldiers, and the generals who commanded the fleet.

When two islands tried to leave the league, the Athenians sent their fleet to punish them. Athens was growing more and more powerful. At first, the league's money was kept on Delos, but in 454 B.C. the Athenians took the treasure to Athens. They said that this was for safekeeping, but it meant that the Athenians could now do whatever they liked with the money.

▼ The marketplace at Delos, where the great meeting of Greek city-states took place. Delos was believed to be the birthplace of the god Apollo. This made it one of the holiest places in the world to the Greeks. It was so important that the much bigger neighboring islands were called the Cyclades, meaning those "around" Delos.

Most of the money was used to pay for the war against Persia. However, the Athenians kept some for their goddess, Athena. This meant that the members of the league were now paying tribute, or tax, to Athens. Little by little, the league had turned into the empire of Athens.

▼ A map of the Athenian Empire about 450 B.C.

BLACK SEA

0   50   100   150   200km
0   50   100 miles

ADRIATIC SEA

Byzantium

Bisanthe

Amphipolis
THASOS
SAMOTHRAKE
IMBROS
LEMNOS

AEGEAN SEA

LESBOS

EUBOIA
Eretria
KHIOS
Kolophon

IONIAN SEA

ATTICA
Salamis
Athens
AIGINE
KEOS
ANDROS
TENOS
SAMOS

Olympia

DELOS
PAROS
NAXOS
KOS

Sparta

MELOS

M E D I T E R R A N E A N   S E A

RHODES

KARPATHOS

The Athenian Empire

CRETE

CHAPTER THREE

THE PLAN FOR THE PARTHENON

▼ The city-states controlled by Athens were forced to stop using their own coins. They had to use Athenian coins, each one showing Athena and her sacred bird, the owl.

By about 450 B.C., the Persians were no longer a threat to Greece. The Athenian war fleet had freed the cities of the eastern Greeks from Persian rule. These cities were forced to join the Athenian Empire, which was now at its most powerful.

Pericles, who was leader of the Athenians, wanted Athens to look like a city that ruled a great empire. Around 450 B.C., Pericles suggested using the money collected from the allies to rebuild the temples that had been burned by the Persians. This money had been given for the war against Persia, and some citizens said it was wrong to use it for any other purpose. Pericles replied: "It is only

fair that after Athens has been equipped with all she needs to carry on the war, she should use the rest for public works, which, once completed, will bring her glory for all time."

Pericles won the argument. The first temple to be planned was a new Parthenon for Athena. It was to be built on the base of the half-finished temple destroyed by the Persians.

The Parthenon was to be the work of the whole city. Hundreds of ordinary citizens, foreign workers, and slaves helped in the actual building work. All the citizens had a role of some kind in the building of the temple. Every decision was discussed in the public meetings, and every single payment had to be approved by the citizens of Athens.

Pericles (499 – 429 B.C.)
Pericles was the man who had led the Athenians to power. He was the most influential of Athenians; almost every year, from 461 B.C. to his death in 429 B.C., he was reelected as general. He was a smart man who knew how to win over the citizens at their public meetings. A poet named Eupolis later remembered Pericles with these words: "He was the greatest speaker of all... He cast a spell on us." According to the Greek historian Plutarch, Pericles had a very long forehead, which is why he is always shown wearing a helmet.

The little temple of Athena Nike (meaning "of victory") on the right, with its Ionic columns. Toward the middle are the Doric columns of the Propylaea, the huge gateway to the Acropolis.

The Greeks had fixed ideas about what a temple was supposed to look like, because they had been building them for hundreds of years. Their earliest temples were made of wood and mud-brick. When the Greeks began to build in stone, about 700 B.C., they copied many of the features of wooden buildings. Even wooden pegs, used to fit larger parts together, were copied in stone.

There were two styles for building temples, which developed in different parts of the Greek world. The Greeks on the mainland invented a simple, sturdy style called Doric. The eastern Greeks invented a more

Optical illusion
Although the Parthenon seems perfectly rectangular (top), it was designed with subtle curves (bottom) that enhance its strength. The bulge of the columns makes them seem more imposing. They also tilt inward as they rise, which exaggerates their height. The columns at the edges are slightly thicker and more closely spaced than the rest—this makes the corners, which stand out against the sky, look stronger.

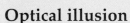

decorative style called Ionic. The easiest way to tell them apart is by looking at the capitals, the tops of the columns. The Ionic capital is decorated with two swirls.

The Athenians used both Doric and Ionic styles of architecture. When they wanted to build a big, imposing structure, they chose the strong Doric style. For smaller temples, they preferred the lighter Ionic style. Both styles are used on the Acropolis.

The Parthenon was designed by two architects named Ictinus and Callicrates. Their aim was not to design a new type of building but to make the most perfect Doric temple possible. They had a strict set of rules to follow about proportions and shapes. They knew what a Doric temple had to look like.

Doric capital

Ionic capital

CHAPTER FOUR

BUILDING THE PARTHENON

Work on the Parthenon began in 447 B.C. It was one of the few Greek buildings to be made completely out of marble. The 22,000 tons of marble used to build the Parthenon came from a quarry on Mount Pentelicus, 10 mi. (16 km) away. The blocks were cut by hand and lowered down the mountainside. They were then taken to Athens on carts pulled by teams of oxen.

▼ Every block and column drum of the Parthenon had to be precisely measured and designed. The individual curves or angles of each piece fitted together to form the final impression of straight lines and immense strength.

At the Acropolis, the stone carvers shaped the marble into drum-shaped blocks for the columns and rectangular blocks for the walls. Every block had to be perfect, because no mortar was used to join them. The wall blocks were fixed with iron clamps, wrapped in lead to keep them from rusting. The drums were joined by a pin set in a hole in the center. Ten or twelve drums were used in each column.

Only the tops and bottoms of the drums were finished before assembly. Once they had been set into place, they were cut back to their final surface. The aim was to make each column look like a single piece of marble.

Building the Parthenon
1. Wall block
2. Scaffolding
3. Lifting tongs
4. Column drum
5. Hoist
6. Oxen bringing stone

These remains on the Acropolis are believed to have been the workshop of Phidias, where he worked on the statue of Athena Parthenos. Phidias went on to make an even more famous ivory and gold statue, of Zeus, king of the gods, which was known as one of the Seven Wonders of the World.

While the walls of the Parthenon were going up, the greatest Athenian artist, Phidias, was busy in his workshop next to the building site. He was making the huge statue of the goddess Athena. It was called Athena Parthenos and would be housed in the new temple.

The statue, which was more than 40 ft. (12 m) high, was made of wood covered with precious materials. The goddess's skin was ivory, using elephant tusks brought by sea from Egypt. Her clothing and armor were made of 200 lbs. (100 kg) of gold. These materials meant that the statue of Athena cost more to make than the whole Parthenon. A great deal of work went into the statue. Athena's face, more than 6.5 ft. (2 m) high, was made out of hundreds of tiny ivory strips. More detail went into her gold shield and sandals, which were covered with pictures of legendary battle scenes.

The statue was placed in the middle of the temple, facing the east door and the rising sun. There was a shallow pool of water just in front of the goddess. This was partly to keep the ivory from cracking in the dry air. But it also reflected the light up onto Athena's face. At sunrise, with her golden dress and white face gleaming with reflected light, the statue must have looked overwhelming.

"The hands of Phidias alone were able to give birth to gods... Those were the good old days for Greece!... When she had an artist unmatched by any that later ages produced; when it was possible to show men how the gods looked."

The Greek writer Philo of Byzantium, about 225 B.C.

▼ Although the Parthenos no longer exists, it was so famous that many smaller versions were made over the centuries. This one in the Museum of Athens is called the Varvakeion. In one hand, she holds a statue of the winged goddess of victory—this figure was as large as a human being on Phidias's original Parthenos.

As well as making the giant statue of Athena, Phidias was in charge of the design of the sculptures that decorated the outside walls of the Parthenon. He had a large team of skilled sculptors to do the actual carving.

There were three types of sculpture on the Parthenon. The first pieces to be carved were the metopes, square blocks carved with scenes of single combat. They showed gods fighting giants, Greeks grappling with centaurs (who were half-horse and half-man), or Amazon warrior women. The sculptors then carved a frieze, which went all the way around the wall of the temple. The last job was to carve enormous statues for the pediments. Each end showed an event in the story of Athena: the east pediment showed her birth, while the western end depicted her contest with Poseidon.

▼ In this 19th-century painting by Sir Lawrence Alma-Tadema, Phidias is standing on scaffolding next to the Parthenon frieze, showing it to the admiring Athenians. You can see the brightly painted band of figures along the building, making their great procession.

The mystery of the Parthenon frieze

The figures of the frieze are taking part in a religious procession to celebrate Athena's birthday. But why are there no hoplites, who would almost certainly have been part of the procession? Why does the frieze show 192 horses and riders that wouldn't have actually been there? Some people believe they represent the 192 soldiers lost at the battle of Marathon. The Greeks believed the souls of dead heroes sometimes rode up to meet the gods on Mount Olympus. There are many theories about what the frieze represents, but the mystery remains.

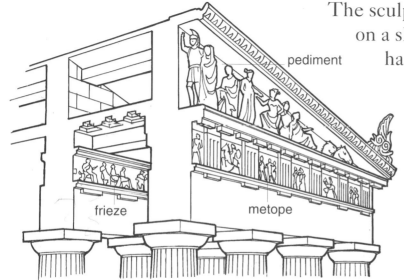

frieze

metope

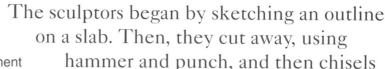

pediment

The sculptors began by sketching an outline on a slab. Then, they cut away, using hammer and punch, and then chisels of various sizes. The surface was sanded and polished, and shining bronze fittings, such as weapons and bridles, were added. The figures were then painted, like all Greek sculpture. Women were shown as pale-skinned, while the men were tanned. This indicated their different ways of life.

The buildings of the Acropolis

1. House of the Arrephoroi
2. The Erectheion
3. The great altar
4. The Parthenon
5. Statue of Athena Promachos
6. The Chalkotheke (bronze store)
7. Sanctuary of Artemis Brauronia
8. Service building
9. Picture gallery
10. The Propylaea
11. Temple of Athena Nike

CHAPTER FIVE

WORSHIP ON THE ACROPOLIS

The Acropolis was a holy place. It was the highest point of the city, where the earth met the heavens, the home of the gods. It had been the religious center of Athens for hundreds of years before the Parthenon was built.

Inside the Parthenon
This 19th-century engraving shows what the interior of the Parthenon would have looked like when it was completed. The Parthenon was the treasury of the Athenian empire. Tribute, war trophies, and offerings to the goddess were all kept in the storeroom behind the statue. The statue itself was seen as a store of gold. The golden armor and clothing were made of plates that could be removed in time of need. The Athenians believed that Athena would be happy to give up the gold if her city needed it.

After the Parthenon was finished in 432 B.C., other new buildings were begun on the Acropolis. These included the Erectheion, which housed the ancient wooden statue of Athena; the little temple to Athena Nike; and a big building, the Propylaea, which acted as the gateway to the Acropolis.

You can still see these buildings if you visit Athens today. Many other features of the ancient Acropolis have disappeared. It was covered with war trophies—armor and weapons captured in war hung everywhere as reminders of Athens' success in war. There was a big bronze statue of Athena Promachos in her armor, also made by Phidias.

"And so the buildings rose up, as imposing in their sheer size as they were graceful, since the artists strove to excel themselves in the beauty of their workmanship. Yet the most wonderful thing about them was the speed with which they were finished. They were created in such a short space of time, to last for all time."

The Greek writer Plutarch, in the second century A.D.

The Erectheion

The Erectheion was the holiest place on the Acropolis, home to the ancient olive wood statue of Athena and a shrine to several gods and early kings. It has a small porch with columns carved in the shape of women, known as the Caryatids. The other porch contains the rock that the ancient Greeks believed was struck by Poseidon in his contest with Athena. Her own sacred olive tree grew just outside.

Temples such as the Parthenon were not places for group worship—they were the homes of the gods whose statues they contained. The actual religious ceremonies, like much of Greek life, took place in the open air.

Throughout the year, the Athenians had many religious festivals. The processions and sacrifices celebrated different gods and involved different rituals. The festival of Artemis, goddess of wild animals, was celebrated with a dance performed by little girls pretending to be bears. During the Panathenaia, Athena's birthday festival, little boys danced holding shields.

The Panathenaia was the biggest and most important festival in Athens. It began with contests: running and chariot races and musical and poetry competitions. Prizes were jars of olive oil, each decorated with a painting of Athena. After the contests was the great procession, when the goddess's new dress was wheeled up to the Acropolis, followed by the animal sacrifices on the great altar.

▲ The priestess of Athena on the right is about to set out two cushioned seats, which her attendants are carrying. This is part of the Parthenon frieze, which depicts the Panathenaic procession on Athena's birthday.

Athena's servant girls

Every year, two little girls, aged between 7 and 11, were chosen to live on the Acropolis. They were called the Arrephoroi, and they were there to keep Athena company and act as her special servants. After a year they went back to their families, and two new girls were sent in their place. It was a great honor to be chosen, but the Acropolis must have been a lonely place at night, when everyone had gone home.

The Greek city-states lost their freedom in 338 B.C., when they were conquered by King Philip of Macedon. Then, in 146 B.C., the Romans arrived. Greece became part of the enormous Roman Empire.

The Parthenon stood unchanged. Phidias's famous statue was visited and admired by Roman tourists. The Athenians still celebrated their goddess's birthday, wheeling their wooden ship up the winding hill of the Acropolis. All this had to stop when Christianity became the official religion of the Roman Empire, in the fourth century A.D. The old gods, including Athena, were now said to be devils. Sacrifice was banned. The statues of the old gods were destroyed.

The Christians had an effective way of winning over people. They would take a Greek temple and turn it into a church, dedicated to a saint who was most like the god who had been worshiped there. Around A.D. 450, the Parthenon became a church, dedicated at first to "Holy Wisdom" and then to the Virgin Mary, mother of Christ. So people now went to the Parthenon to pray to the Virgin of Athens rather than to Athena the Virgin.

To turn the temple into a church, changes had to be made. Unlike a temple, a church was a place for group worship. The religious ceremonies took place inside the building rather than outside by an altar. In order to hold the worshipers, the two rooms were made into one. At the eastern end, an apse, a curved extension to house the Christian altar, was added. The inside was richly decorated with religious paintings. The ceiling was given a great mosaic, a picture made up of tiny tiles showing the Virgin Mary.

▲ A 19th-century engraving showing the Roman army as they invaded and conquered the Greeks in 146 B.C.

▶ A 14th-century Greek mosaic of the Virgin Mary, who had taken over from Athena as the Virgin of Athens. The Parthenon was a Christian church for a thousand years, 150 years longer than it had been Athena's temple.

In the Middle Ages, Athens passed from one foreign ruler to another. The city was captured by the French (1205); then the Catalans from Spain (1311); then the Florentines of Italy (1385). These invading peoples were all Christian, and the Parthenon continued to serve as their church.

Everything changed when the Turks arrived, capturing Athens in 1458 after a two-year siege. The Turks converted the Parthenon into a mosque, a Muslim place for prayer. They whitewashed over the Christian wall paintings, for Muslims did not approve of art showing

▶ The Turks were Muslims, followers of the religion of Islam. From the 1320s, they had been fighting a holy war against the Christians of Greece. Under their greatest leader, Sultan Mehmed the Conqueror (right), they swept across the Greek territories, conquering the cities of Constantinople in 1453 and Athens in 1458.

▲ A drawing from the 16th century showing how the Parthenon looked during the 200 years it served as a mosque. You can see the minaret that was built onto the roof by the Turks.

human figures. In spite of this they left the original Greek sculptures undamaged, perhaps because they were so difficult to reach. On the outside of the building, the Turks added a minaret, a tall tower from which the faithful were called to prayer. The voice of a muezzin sang out five times a day from the minaret: "Come to prayer! Come to security! God is most great!" The Turks further altered the appearance of the Acropolis by building several small houses around the temples.

By the 1600s, Athens had shrunk into a small and unimportant town. It was now that the first wealthy European travelers began to arrive, as tourists. They had read about the Parthenon in books by ancient Greek and Roman writers. They wanted to see if the temple lived up to its descriptions, and they were not disappointed. Most of the sculptures were well preserved. The milky-white marble still sparkled.

"The most beautiful piece of antiquity remaining in the world."

George Wheler, a British visitor to the Parthenon in 1682

CHAPTER SIX

THE PARTHENON BESIEGED

▼ In the explosion of 1687 the roof of the the Parthenon, most of its inner walls, and the tops of the middle columns at the side were all destroyed. A fire burned on the Acropolis for two days before it could be put out.

In September 1687, the city of Athens was besieged yet again. The attacking army came from Venice in Italy. The Venetians hoped to drive the Turks out of Greece and conquer the country for themselves.

Outnumbered, the Turkish defenders moved up onto the Acropolis. They hoped that the Venetians would not fire

VEDUTA DEL CAST: D'ACROPOLIS DALLA PARTE DI TRAMONTANA

directly at the temple with its famous sculptures. So they stored their gunpowder inside, and the women and children sheltered there.

General Francesco Morosini cared only about taking the city. He found out where the gunpowder was stored and ordered his men to fire their cannon at the Parthenon. On the evening of September 26, the whole city was shaken by a deafening explosion. It killed 300 people, and the Turks surrendered. The Parthenon, which had survived for more than 2,000 years, was in ruins.

Venetian vandalism
The Venetians held onto Athens for less than seven months before they abandoned the city. Morosini did further damage to the Parthenon when he tried to remove the central statues on the western end to take back as souvenirs to Venice. His clumsy workers dropped them, smashing them to bits.

▼ The Turks returned to Athens after the Venetians left and found the Parthenon in ruins. It could no longer be used as a mosque. The Turks took stones from the temple to build a little mosque inside its walls, which is shown in this 19th-century painting.

▼ The Elgin Room at the British Museum in 1819. Lord Elgin had brought back half the frieze showing the religious procession, 15 of the metopes showing single combat, and 20 of the big statues of gods from the pediments.

Foreign visitors still went to admire what was left of the Parthenon. Some found bits of sculpture lying on the ground and took them away as souvenirs. The greatest souvenir hunter of all was the wealthy Earl of Elgin, who was fascinated by ancient Greek art and architecture.

In 1799, when he was ambassador to Turkey, Elgin discovered that the Turks were not taking care of the Parthenon and its sculptures. He obtained permission to remove "pieces of stone with old inscriptions and figures" from the Acropolis. This may have meant only that Elgin could take stones that were lying around on the ground. But Elgin used the permission to start sawing

off carvings still on the temple. In 1807 these sculptures were shipped to Great Britain and went on show in London.

In 1816, Lord Elgin sold the Parthenon carvings to the government, and they were moved to the British Museum. Everyone rushed to see the "Elgin Marbles," as they were now called. They were the best examples of Greek art that anyone had seen. A painter, Henry Fuseli, shouted excitedly, "By God! The Greeks were gods!"

Greek art hits the West

When the Elgin Marbles arrived in Great Britain, there was already a growing taste for Greek art. People admired it because of its "ideal beauty." The Greeks only showed the human body at its most perfect. Every country wanted to get its hands on ancient Greek art. The keenest collectors were the Germans, the French, and the British. In the early 1800s, more Greek temples were stripped of their statues, and these ended up in museums in Paris, Munich, Berlin, and London.

▲ In the 19th century, Greek architecture had a huge influence across the Western World. Grand public buildings, such as libraries, law courts and museums, were modeled on Greek temples like the Parthenon. The British Museum, in London, where the Elgin Marbles are housed, is such a building.

CHAPTER SEVEN

RESTORING THE PARTHENON

▶ The Battle of Navarino took place on October 20, 1827. The aim of the allies (Great Britain, France, and Russia) was to put pressure on the Turks to make peace. In the battle, 53 Turkish ships were sunk without a single allied loss.

In 1837, the Greeks formed an Archaeological Society to look after the ancient buildings. Anything on the Acropolis that was not ancient was pulled down. The little temple of Athena Nike was rebuilt, and some of the fallen columns of the Parthenon were repaired. Meanwhile, at the foot of the Acropolis, a modern city began to grow.

In the 1820s, when the Parthenon sculptures were causing a sensation in western Europe, dramatic events were taking place in Greece. After 400 years of Turkish rule, the Greeks were fighting for their freedom.

It was a long and bloody war. To stop the fighting and help the Greeks, the governments of Great Britain, France, and Russia sent a combined fleet of 27 warships to southern Greece. At the Battle of Navarino in 1827, they destroyed the entire Turkish war fleet. By 1830, the Greeks were a free people.

The ancient ruins of the Acropolis were important to the new Greek nation as a reminder of their glorious past. It was because of this that Athens, a little town of 300 houses, was chosen to be the new capital.

"These stones are more precious than rubies... It is to these stones that we owe our rebirth as a nation."

Iakovos Neroulos, president of the Greek Archaeological Society, speaking in 1837 at the ruins of the Parthenon

In the early 1800s, an Englishman named John Cam Hobhouse was traveling in western Greece, at that time still ruled by the Turks. He met an old Greek man who said to him: "You English are carrying off the works of the Greeks, our forefathers. Look after them well. Greeks will come and ask for them back."

Ever since Greece became a free nation in 1830, the Greeks have asked for the Parthenon sculptures to be returned to Athens. From time to time, British people have also called for their return. However, the British Museum has refused to give back the marbles. Like many European museums, the British Museum is filled with foreign works of art. If it returned one object to its country of origin, it might have to return them all.

▼ These sculptures from the Parthenon pediment are displayed at the British Museum. The damaged figures include the goddesses Demeter and Persephone, originally part of an enormous scene depicting Athena's birth from the head of Zeus.

Today Athens, like most modern cities, has a bad problem with pollution. In the hot summer, the fumes from cars and smokestacks make a dense smog that hangs over the city. This eats away at the marble on the Acropolis. In winter, acid rain attacks the stones. As long as these problems remain, the statues cannot be put back on the walls of the Parthenon. However, the Greeks hope that one day they will get the sculptures back and display them in a museum by the Acropolis, placing copies on the temple itself.

"The Parthenon marbles are to the Greek nation a thousand times more dear and more important than they can ever be to the English nation, which simply bought them."

Frederic Harrison, 1890, in a newspaper article entitled "Give Back the Elgin Marbles"

▲ The Parthenon is still under restoration. The skin of the marble, which has been eroded by traffic fumes and acid rain, is being patched. Metal rods, used to repair the columns 150 years ago, have rusted and are being replaced. Those rods that survived the 1687 explosion, made by the ancient Greeks 2,500 years ago, have lasted much better.

TIME LINE

700–501 B.C.

c 700 First stone temples built by the Greeks

500–451 B.C.

490 Persians invade Greece and are defeated at Marathon by the Athenians

498–80 Athenians begin building the first Parthenon

480 Persians invade Greece again, sacking Athens and burning the temples on the Acropolis. The Athenian fleet defeats the Persians at Salamis

478 League of Delos formed by Athens and other states to fight Persia

460 Phidias builds a 90 foot- (27m) high bronze statue of Athena to stand on the Acropolis in the open air

450–401 B.C.

447 Building of a new Parthenon begins on the base of the old one

438 Phidias's gold and ivory statue of Athena set up inside the Parthenon, which is complete, apart from the statues in the pediments

438–432 Carving of the statues of the gods for the pediments

430–404 War between Athens and Sparta, ending with the defeat of Athens

400 B.C.–A.D. 199

338 King Philip of Macedon conquers Greece

146 B.C. Greece becomes part of the Roman Empire

A.D. 200–1299   **A.D. 1300–1599**   **A.D. 1600–1799**   **A.D. 1800–2000**

390 Christianity becomes the only religion allowed in the Roman Empire

c 450 Parthenon converted into a Christian church

1205 Athens captured by the Franks, or French

1311 Franks driven out by the Catalans, from southern Spain

1385 Catalans driven out by the Florentines, from Italy

1456–8 Turks capture Athens and lay siege to the Acropolis, which eventually surrenders

c 1460 Parthenon converted into a Muslim mosque

1687 Athens besieged by the Venetians. They fire cannons at the Parthenon, where the Turks kept their gunpowder, and cause a terrible explosion

1688 Turks return to Athens

1801 Lord Elgin begins to remove carvings from the Parthenon

1821-30 Greeks fight against the Turks for their freedom

1834 Athens becomes capital of the kingdom of Greece

1836–42 Temple of Athena Nike rebuilt

1984 Work begins on the restoration of the Parthenon

GLOSSARY

Acropolis
High city. Most Greek cities had an acropolis, a place to take refuge if the city was attacked, and also the site of the city's main temples.

Altar
A flat-topped block or platform, usually outside a temple, where offerings to a god were made.

Antiquity
Something belonging to ancient times.

Citizens
People who have full rights as members of a particular state. In ancient Greece, only men could be citizens.

Decree
An order made by a person in a position of power or by an authority such as a government or council.

Festival
A celebration. Greek festivals were always in honor of their gods. They were marked by sports, drama, music, and animal sacrifice.

Frieze
A continuous band of pictures.

Ivory
The hard, toothlike substance from which animal tusks are formed. Elephant ivory is still used to make decorative objects, although in many parts of the world killing elephants for their ivory is against the law.

Muezzin
The man who calls Muslims to prayer.

Relief
An image that is carved or molded to stand out from its background.

Rites
A sequence of actions and words that is always done in the same way on a particular occasion, such as a religious sacrifice or baptism.

Sacrifice
The killing of an animal as an offering to a god.

Trident
A spear with three points.

FURTHER INFORMATION

BOOKS

Gardner, Robert. *Architecture.* Yesterday's Science, Today's Technology. New York: 21st Century Books, 1994.

Lerner Geography Dept. Staff, ed. *Greece in Pictures.* Visual Geography. Minneapolis, MN: Lerner Group, 1992.

Loverance, Rowena. *Ancient Greece.* See Through History. New York: Viking Children's Books, 1993.

Pratt, Paula B. *Architecture.* World History. San Diego: Lucent Books, 1995.

Singer Donna. *Structures That Changed the Way the World Looked.* Twenty Events. Austin, TX: Raintree Steck-Vaughn, 1994.

Williams, A. Susan. *The Greeks.* Look Into the Past. New York: Thomson Learning, 1993.

Picture acknowledgments

The publishers would like to thank the following for allowing their pictures to be reproduced: Lesley and Roy Adkins: pages 24, 43; Ancient Art & Architecture Collection: pages 4, 6, 8 (bottom), 11, 13 (top and bottom), 14 (top), 16–17, 25, 29; Bridgeman Art Library: pages 26 (Birmingham City Museums and Art Gallery), 37 (The Fine Art Society), 42 (British Museum); British Museum: pages 35, 38; C M Dixon Photo Resources: pages 7, 14–15, 18, 22; Mary Evans Picture Library: pages 32, 40; Werner Forman Archive: pages 33, 34 ; Michael Holford Photographs: pages 8 (top), 9, 10, 19, 20–21, 27, 31; Tony Stone Images: front cover (Vic Thomasson), pages 30, 39, 40–41; Wayland Picture Library: pages 3, 12, 44, 45.

INDEX